ABSOLUTE BEGINNERS
Keyboard

AMSCO PUBLICATIONS

London/New York/Paris/Sydney/Copenhagen/Madrid

Exclusive Distributors:
Music Sales Corporation
257 Park Avenue South
New York, NY 10010 USA.

Music Sales Limited
8/9 Frith Street,
London W1D 3JB, England.

Music Sales Pty Limited
120 Rothschild Avenue,
Rosebery, NSW 2018, Australia.

Order No. AM 92618
ISBN 0.7119.7430.6

Arranged by Jeff Hammer
Model: Arthur Dick
Keyboard and stool kindly loaned by Rose Morris
Cover and text photographs by George Taylor
Other photographs courtesy of LFI/Redferns
Book design by Chloë Alexander

Printed in United States of America by
Vicks Lithograph and Printing Corporation

Contents

Introduction

Welcome to *Absolute Beginners for Keyboard*. Whether you're a budding pianist or the owner of a new keyboard, this book will get you started, and get you playing, fast! We'll teach you the essential basics that all keyboard players need to know.

This book will guide you from the very first time you sit down at the keyboard through to playing whole pieces confidently with both hands together.

Easy-to-follow instructions
will guide you through

- correct posture and playing position
- finding your way around the keyboard
- reading basic musical notation, learning note names and understanding rhythm
- playing with hands separately and together

Play along with the backing track as you learn—the specially recorded audio will let you hear how the music *should* sound—then try playing the part yourself.

Practice regularly and often. Twenty minutes every day is far better than two hours on the weekend with nothing in between. Not only are you training your brain to understand how to play the keyboard, you are also teaching your muscles to memorize certain repeated actions.

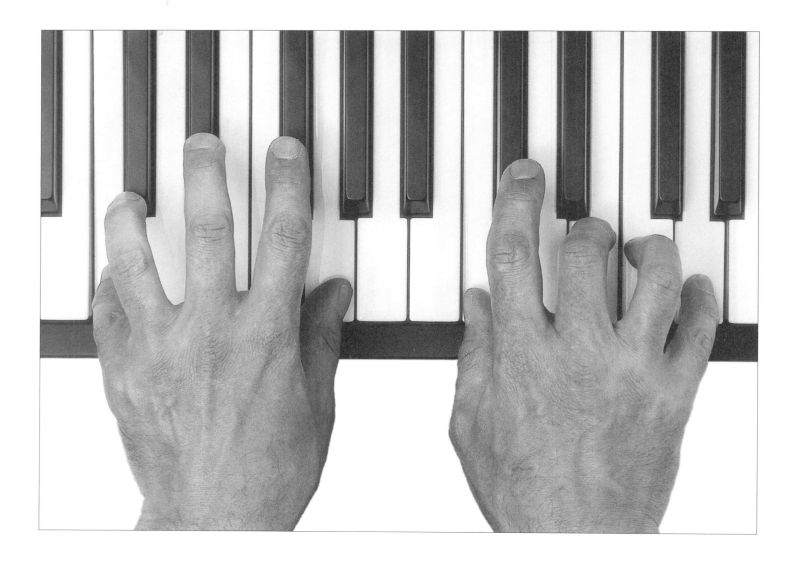

Playing position

A good playing position means that you'll be comfortable at the keyboard, and, more importantly, you'll be more likely to play well.

Sit facing the middle of the keyboard with your feet opposite the pedals and try to keep a reasonably straight back. Avoid tension in any part of your body, particularly in your lower arms.

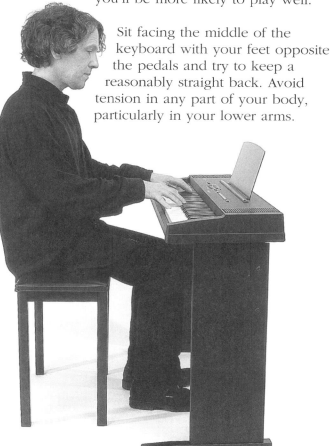

Make sure you don't slump over the keyboard.

X

Tip

An adjustable piano stool is better than an ordinary chair, because it allows people of differing statures to play in comfort. Make sure your seat is at a height which allows your lower arms to sit level with, or just above, the keys.

Fingering

Fingering is a system designed to prevent your fingers getting tangled up in knots. It works like this:

Each finger is given a number, as shown in the photograph below.

You will see these numbers over the notes in the music—they tell you which fingers to use for those notes.

Try to stick to the recommended fingerings for each piece and you will soon assume the habit of having your hands in the correct position.

CHECKPOINT

WHAT YOU'VE ACHIEVED SO FAR...

You can now:
- Sit at the keyboard in the correct position
- Place your hands on the keyboard correctly
- Understand right and left hand fingerings

Left hand

Right hand

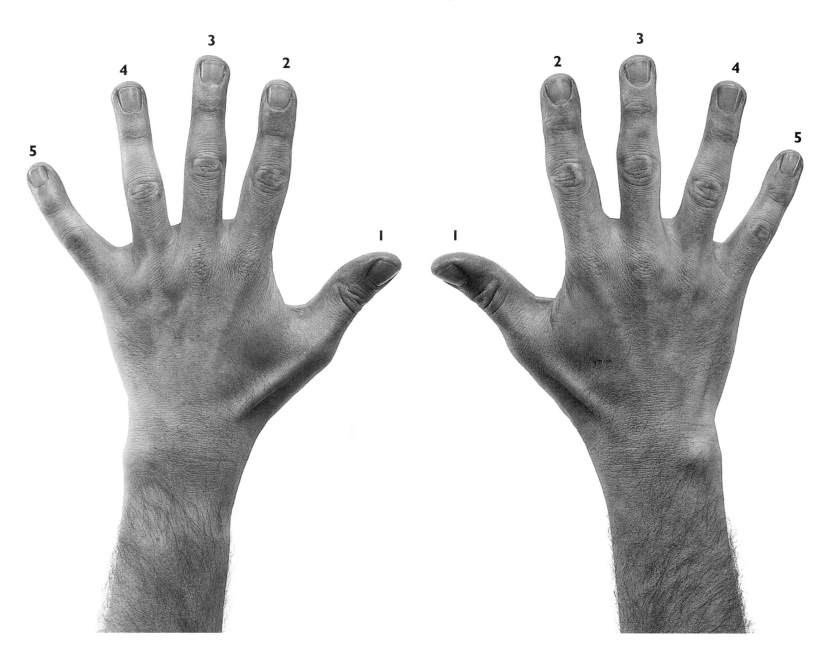

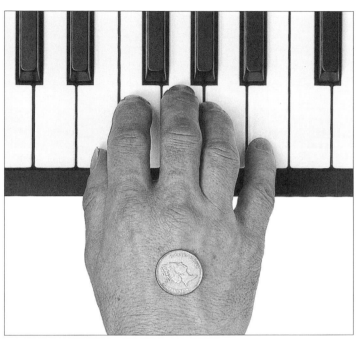

Tip

Try resting a small coin on the back of your hand as you place your hands on the keyboard. You should be able to play quite comfortably without the coin falling off!

Your hands should be supported from the wrist—it's very important that you don't permit your wrists to descend below the keyboard.

Now, with your fingers sitting lightly above the keys, curl your fingers slightly as if gently holding an imaginary ball.

Your fingertips should cover five adjacent notes in each hand. This is the normal five finger position, to which your hand will eventually return automatically.

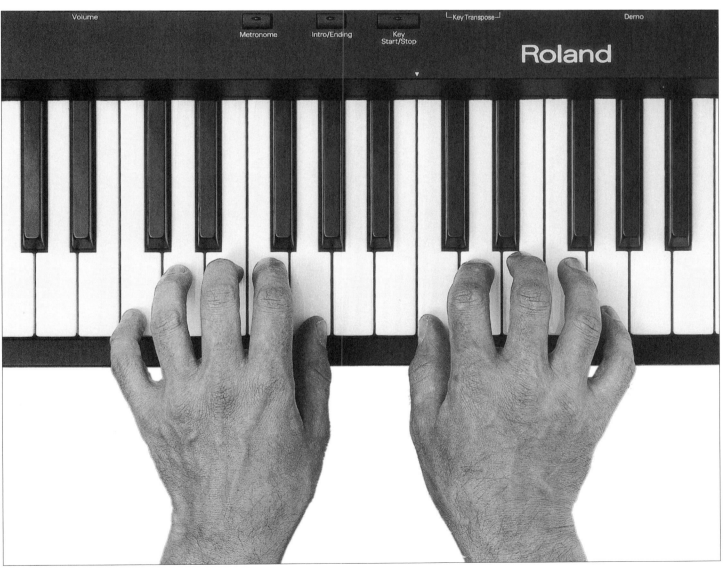

Finding your way around

At first glance, the keyboard may seem confusing—so many notes! But the keyboard is actually just the same series of 12 notes repeated over and over, for its entire length!

Only seven letter names are used. The black keys are arranged in twos and threes in a repeating pattern—this irregularity is actually very useful, because it enables you to find your way around the keyboard.

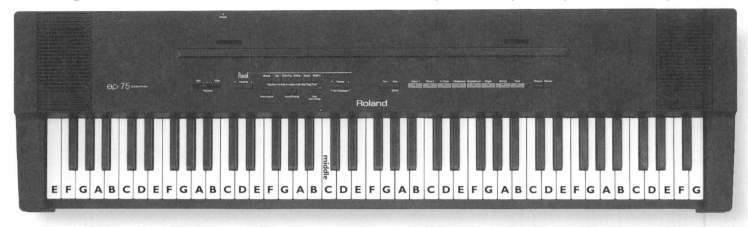

This is the section that we deal with in this book:

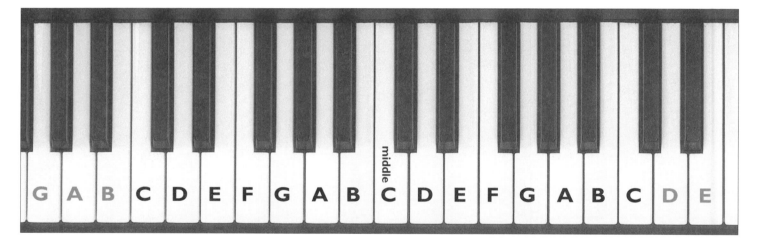

Reading Music

Reading music is easy—once you understand the fundamentals you'll take to it in no time.

There are two basic elements to the way music is written: *pitch* and *duration*. Pitch tells you how high or low a note is (low is to the left on the keyboard, high is to the right), and duration tells you how long the note is played for, and when it is played in relation to other notes around it.

The five lines on which the notes are placed are called a *staff*. A note placed on top of the staff is higher than a note placed at the bottom.

For keyboard players there is a staff for the left hand and one for the right. In the early part of the book we will concern ourselves with the right hand only.

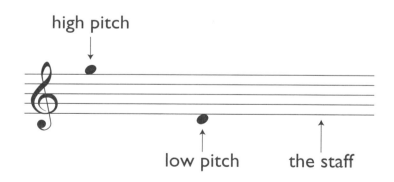

Jargon Buster

Duration—how long a note lasts
Pitch—how high or low a note is
Staff—the five lines on which music is written

If you look at any piece of music you can see that notes have different shapes – some have tails, some have solid note heads, while others are hollow. They will soon become very familiar to you.

This symbol **o** is called a *whole note* and lasts for the duration of a full bar, so it has a count of four beats. Against the count of 1 – 2 – 3 – 4 you would count whole notes like this:

Music has a basic pulse or *beat*; multiples of these beats are grouped into larger units called *bars* or *measures*.

Bars are made up of groups of beats – when you tap your foot to a piece of music, you're responding to the beat.

The most common grouping of beats is 4 in a bar: called 'common time,' and we'll be using this initially.

Try counting steadily from 1 to 4 and then repeating that sequence:

1 – 2 – 3 – 4 / 1 – 2 – 3 – 4 / 1 – 2 – 3 – 4 / etc

Each time you count '1' you are beginning a new bar.

1	2	3	4	1	2	3	4	1	2	3	4	etc.

This symbol ♩ is called a *half note* and lasts for two beats, so it is counted like this:

1	2	3	4	1	2	3	4	1	2	3	4	etc.

Finally, this symbol ♩ is called a *quarter note* and lasts for one beat. Thus there are four of these to every bar and they are counted like this:

1	2	3	4	1	2	3	4	1	2	3	4	etc.

You now know enough about rhythm to play some music.

Your first note

Finding Middle C

The easiest way to locate a white key is to see where it fits into the pattern of black keys.

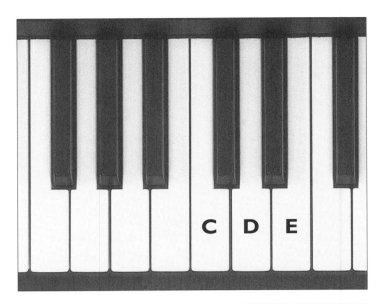

Look for the groups of two black keys, and then find the white key in the middle of these. This note is **D**. **C** is directly to the left of D—or to the left of the group of two black keys.

The groups of black keys are repeated all the way up the keyboard so there are lots of Cs. In order to distinguish between them we usually refer to one of them as *middle C*, which is—you guessed it—the one closest to, or in the center of the keyboard.

See the photo below and then locate middle C on your keyboard.

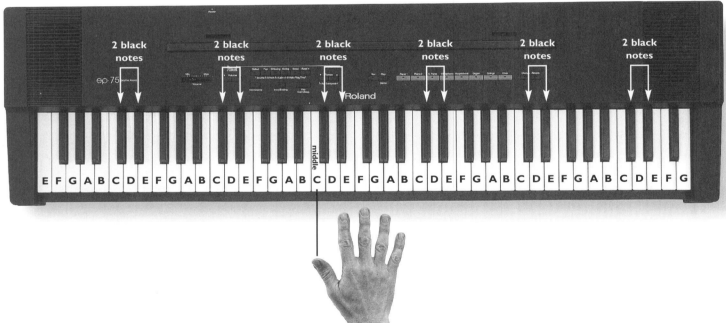

This is how middle C looks on the staff:

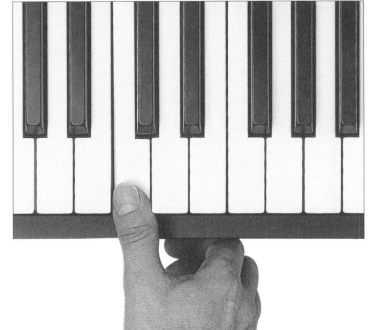

Notice that middle C occupies a small line directly under the main staff. This is called a *leger line*. Leger lines enable us to write notes which are higher or lower than the staff's five lines and four spaces. It is important to be able to recognize one C from another, otherwise you may play the right notes (according to their name) but on the wrong part of the keyboard!

The examples on the next few pages all use middle C and the notes just above it.

Now you're ready to play your first piece.

Don't worry about reading music—as long as you can count to four and you can remember where C is, then you can play this piece.

Now for the first piece. After the four beat intro click, play a C for four beats with the accompanying music, then rest for four beats, then play for four and rest for four, and so on until the end of the piece.

This piece lasts for 8 bars; this equals 8 counts of four in total. This may seem simple, but already you are teaching yourself the discipline of playing in time, and how to count rests. These skills become more crucial as your playing develops.

Learning to count regular beats is something which will become second nature to you eventually. Play this exercise a few times at differing speeds, starting very slowly and gradually increasing the tempo. Smooth, regular and controlled playing is what you should be aiming for at this point.

Track 1 on the CD demonstrates how this should sound, and **Track 2** gives you a backing track that you can play along with.

Count: 1 2 3 4   1 2 3 4   1 2 3 4   1 2 3 4   etc.

The notes D and E

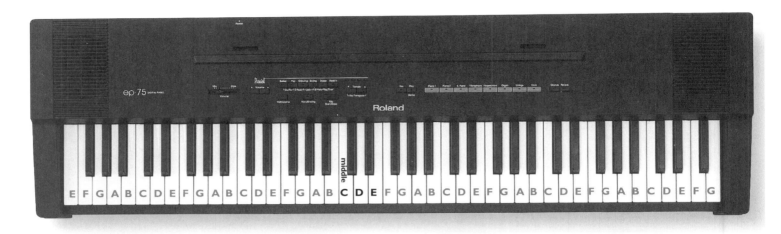

Here is the note **D** which you first found in between the groups of 2 black notes. Make sure you play the one directly to the right of middle C.

D

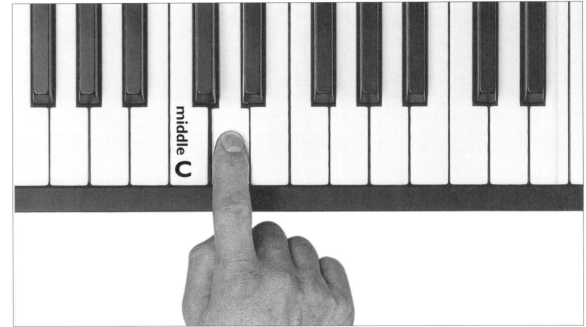

On one side of the note D you found C—on the other side is the note **E**.

E

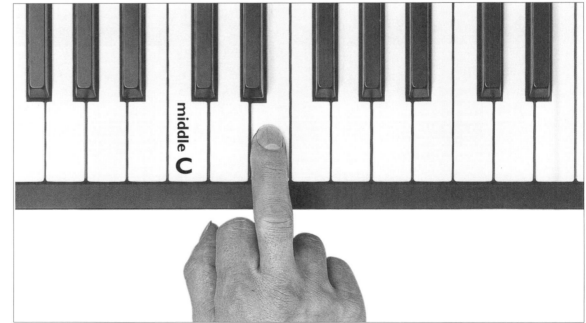

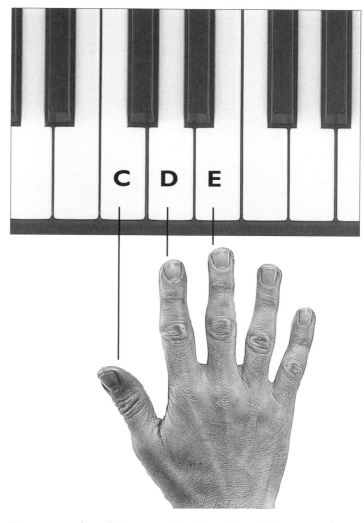

Tip

Try playing all the groups of C, D, E on the keyboard.
Play them and name them out loud as you go.

Below is a tune to help you learn where these notes are. Play C with the thumb on your right hand, and D and E with your index and middle fingers respectively.

The fingering numbers should help you to remember which fingers to use—refer back to the diagram on page 6 if you are unsure.

You don't have to be able to read the music to play this exercise, just speak aloud the names of the notes as you play them. Allow four beats (one bar) per note.

Tip

Keep the tempo slow to start with, gradually increasing speed as you become more confident.

Watch out for the one bar rest after each group of three notes. The count written over the music should help you with the rhythm, while the names of the notes are written underneath the staff.

Listen to the exercise first on **Track 3**, then play along with the backing on **Track 4**.

Keep your hand in a good, relaxed position, avoiding tension in any part of your body, especially the shoulders, lower arms and hands.

As you play each note, press gently but firmly into the keys with a positive finger action.

This piece lasts for 16 bars—try to count them as you play.

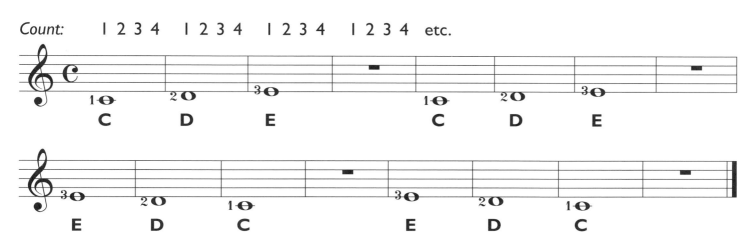

The notes **F, G, A & B**

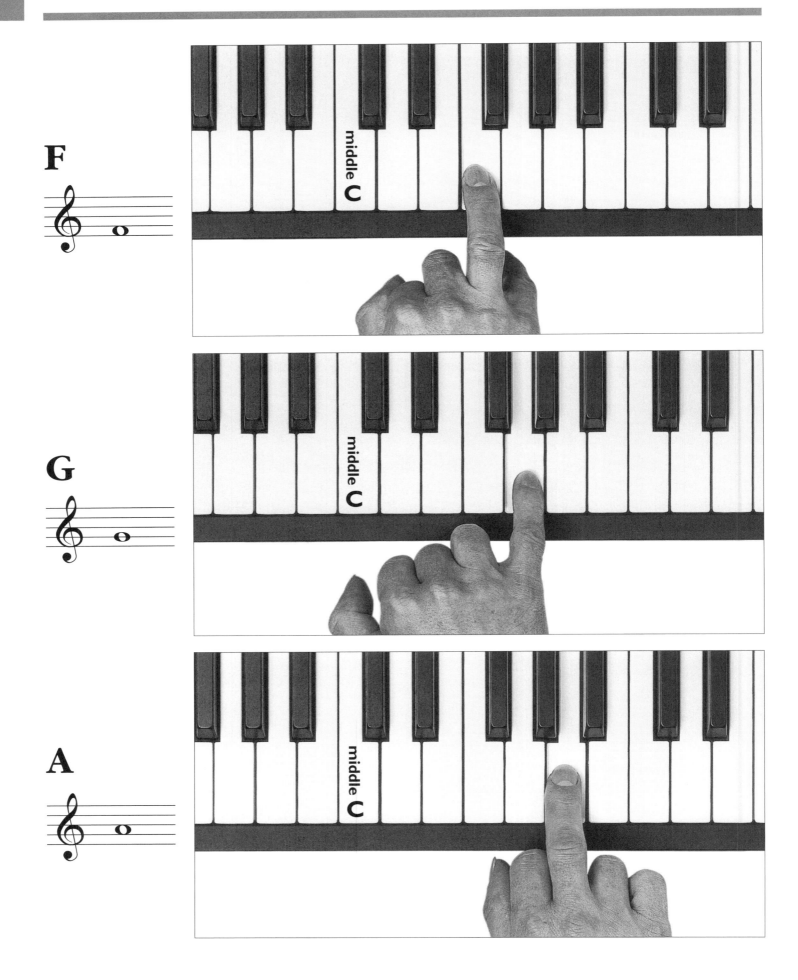

F

G

A

Look at the keyboard below and notice the repeating pattern of three black keys—you can use these to find the white keys around and between them.

Reading from the left, they are **F**, **G**, **A** and **B**. Practice finding each note and say the letter name out loud as you play the note.

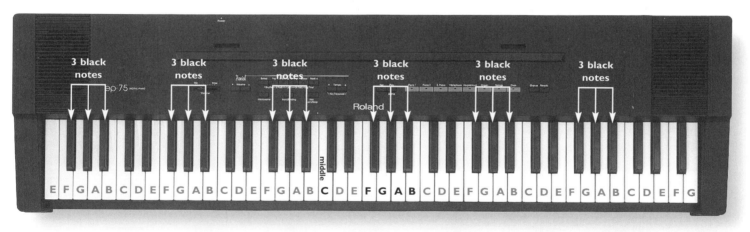

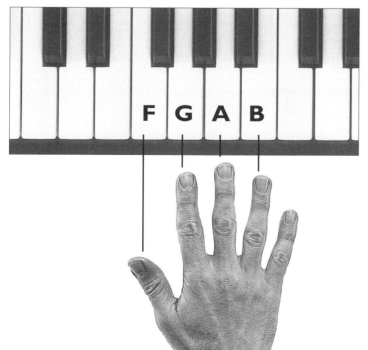

Tip

If you're having trouble memorizing the names and locations of all the notes, try placing labelled stickers onto the keys.

Playing **F, G, A & B**

Now that you are familiar with counting beats and bars, let's try an exercise that familiarizes you with these four new notes, while also teaching you to count in units of two beats each.

For this exercise play the lower note F with the thumb of your right hand, keeping the relaxed hand position you learned earlier.

Keep your other fingers 'hovering' over the other notes.

Listen to the demonstration on **Track 5**, and then try playing along with the backing on **Track 6**.

Tip
The notes in this exercise change after two beats, so you have to think a little quicker than in the previous examples.

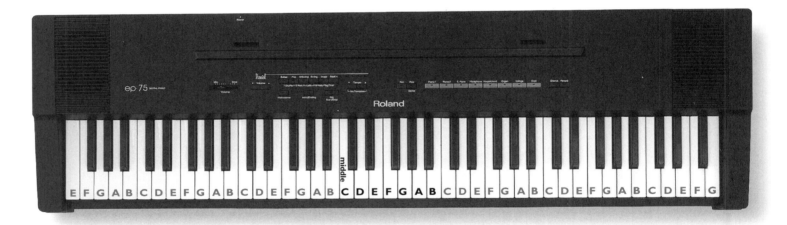

Count: 1 2 3 4   1 2 3 4   1 2 3 4   1 2 3 4 etc.

F G A B   F G A B   F G A B   F G A B

E F G A B C D E F G A B C D E F G A B C D E F G A B C D E F G A B C D E F G A B C D E F G

Right hand summary
You have now learned seven notes in the right hand! Take a moment to make sure you are familiar with them—their names, position on the staff, and location on the keyboard.

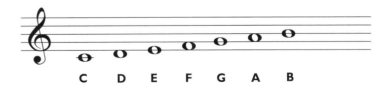

C   D   E   F   G   A   B

CHECKPOINT
WHAT YOU'VE ACHIEVED SO FAR...

You can now:
• Play seven notes
• Understand basic concepts of pitch and rhythm
• Read music from the staff

How can we use the same five lines (staff) for the notes in the right hand and for the different (lower) notes in the left?

The answer lies in the symbol at the beginning of the music. This is called a *clef* (from the French for *key*).

For the left hand we use a bass clef:

And in the right hand we use a treble clef:

These different *clefs* represent the letters **G** and **F**, and their placement on the staff tells us where these notes are situated in each clef.

With the bass clef the two dots to the right of the symbol, placed either side of the second line down from the top, represent the horizontal line of the note F.

This fixes the position of the note F—from this we can work out the positions of the other notes.

Jargon Buster

Treble clef—symbol used on the staff for the right hand
Bass clef—symbol used on the staff for the left hand

Look at how the treble clef curls around the second line up from the bottom of the staff. This fixes the position of the note G—from this we can work out the positions of the surrounding notes.

F

G

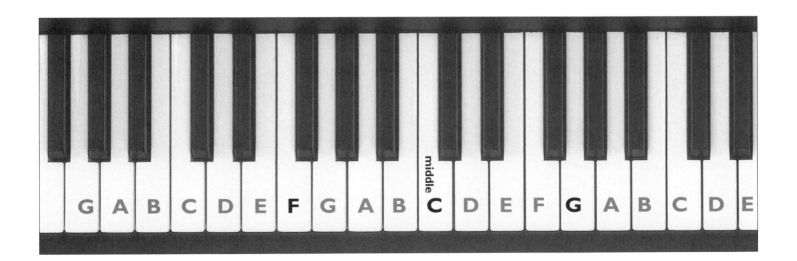

The left-hand notes

Here's how the notes in the bass clef are located. You will see that the rule of all the Cs being immediately to the left of the two black notes still applies—we just write them differently on the staff.

C

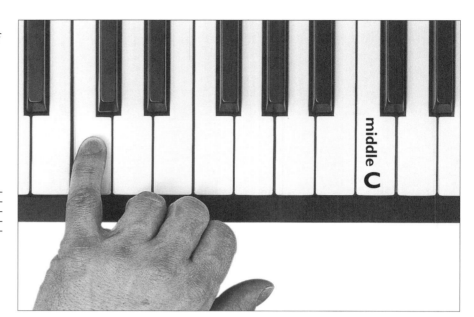

D

E

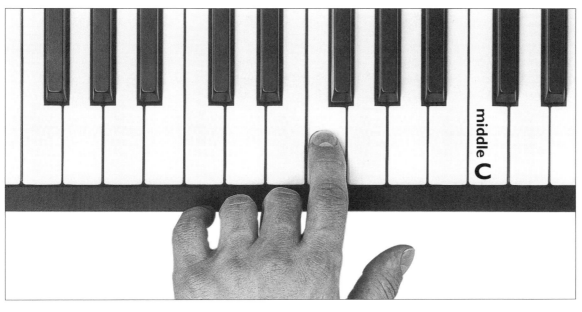

F

G

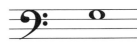

C   D   E   F   G

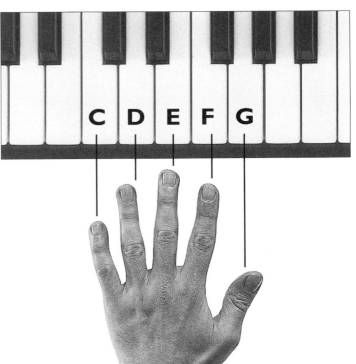

Tip

From now on we will show all the notes on both staffs, with treble and bass clefs.

Playing notes and rests

Here's an exercise designed to get you used to playing with the left hand.

Look out for this symbol ▬ —it's called a rest. It tells you to leave a silent gap of four beats. Count them when you're not playing just as carefully as when you are—that way you will always stay in time.

Listen to the demonstration on **Track 7**, and then try playing along with the backing on **Track 8**.

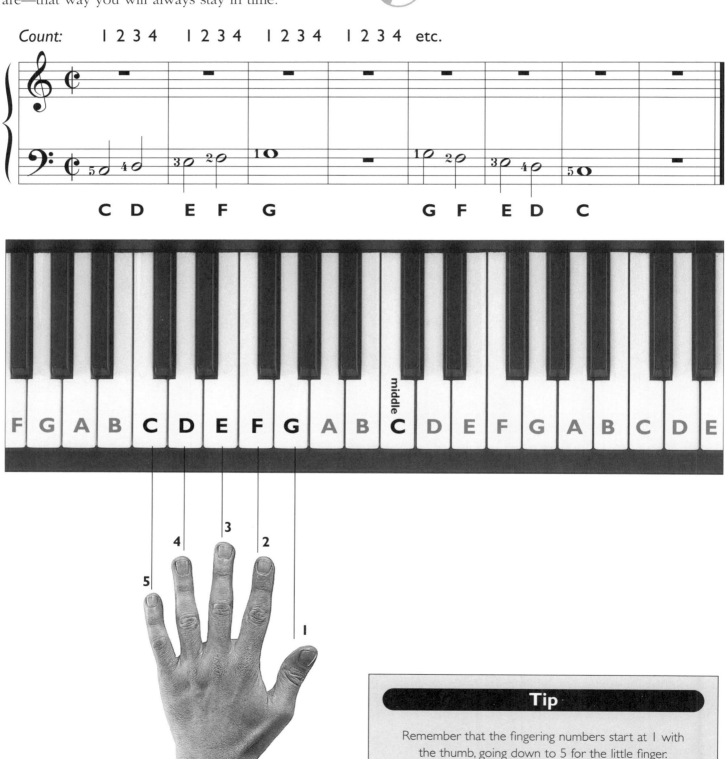

Tip

Remember that the fingering numbers start at 1 with the thumb, going down to 5 for the little finger.

Here's another exercise aimed at getting you to play notes several steps apart in the left hand. Bass lines often move like this, so it is important that you train your left hand to move in this way. If you keep your hand position correct and follow the fingering numbers, this piece will soon fall under your fingers.

Listen to the demonstration on **Track 9**, and then try playing along with the backing on **Track 10**.

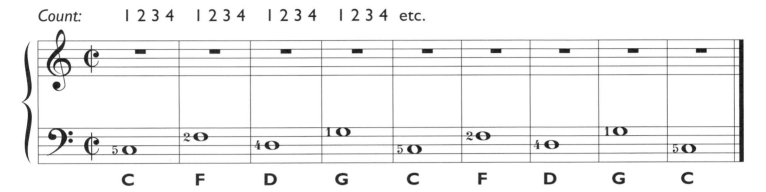

You will have noticed that the bass line moves in intervals (or distances) of four notes: C-F and D-G.

These intervals are known as fourths because there are four notes separating the top and bottom notes. Similarly, if the top and bottom notes are five notes apart, is an interval of a fifth. Bass lines often move in this way.

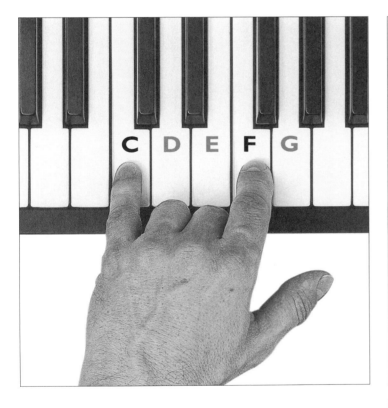

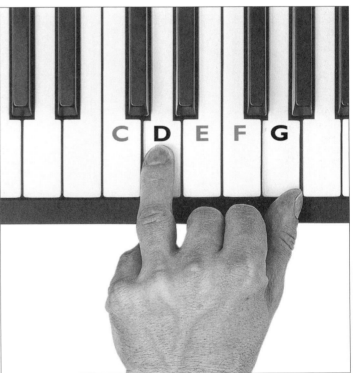

CHECKPOINT

WHAT YOU'VE ACHIEVED SO FAR...

You can now:
- Count and read different rhythms
- Recognize treble and bass clefs
- Use both your left and right hands

Left and right hands together

Now you know enough about keyboard playing to use both your right and left hands together.

There are various things to look out for in this piece:

With two hands playing at once it's more important than ever that you keep your hands and fingers in the correct positions. Use the fingerings given, as they will help to minimize the movement of your hands over the keyboard. In the last bar of the piece you only play for one beat—the remainder of the bar is filled with rests.

And what are those loops joining the last bar to the one before? They are called ties, and they literally 'tie' or 'add' the value of one note to another.

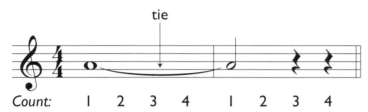

In this case, your left hand doesn't restrike the C in the last bar; you simply hold it down for one extra beat.

So the last C in the left hand starts in bar 7 and lasts for five beats (four + one); and the E in the right hand lasts for three beats (two + one).

Take your time with this exercise—make sure you are confident with it at various tempos before moving on.

Now that you are familiar with the note names in the left and right hands we'll remove the 'safety net' of putting the note names immediately below the music.

Listen to the demonstration on **Track 11**, and then try playing along with the backing on **Track 12.**

▼ Here's where your hands should be, ready to start playing.

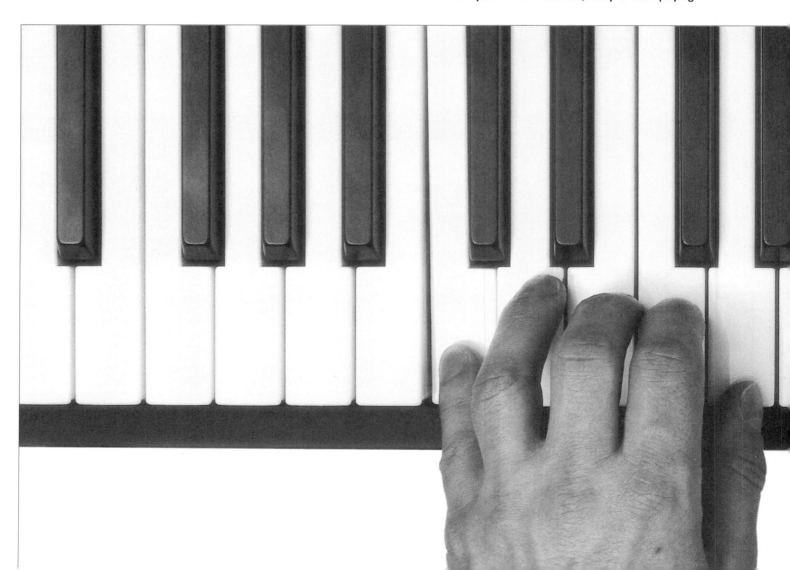

Take a rest!

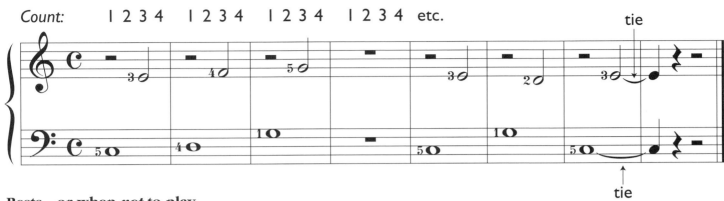

Rests—or when *not* to play.

Now we will look at what the music tells us when you are not playing. The symbols occupying the spaces where you are not playing are called *rests*, and they have similar rhythmic values to notes. This is how they work:

A rest for a whole note or four beats is written like this:

A shorter rest for a half note (equal in length to two beats) looks like this:

A quarter note rest, for a duration of one beat, looks like this:

You can combine these rests. For example, to have a part silent for three beats you would combine the two beat half note rest ▬ with the one beat quarter note rest ❭ giving a total of three beats rest, like this:

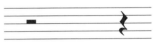

Left hand summary

Well done! You now know seven notes in the right hand, and five notes in the left hand.

To sum up, play through each note slowly, reminding yourself of the note name and its relation to the staff and the keyboard.

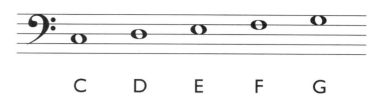

C   D   E   F   G

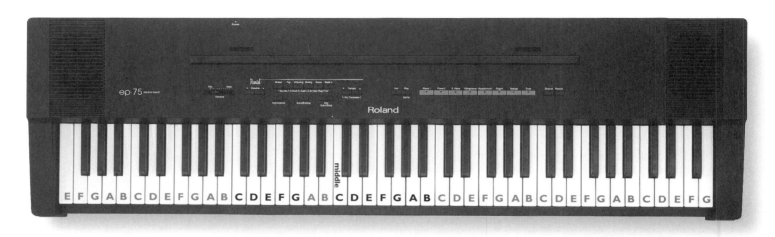

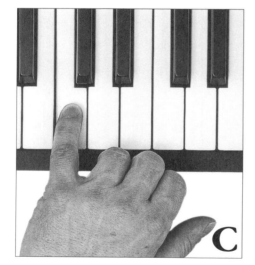

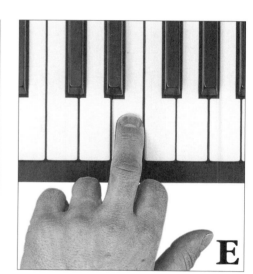

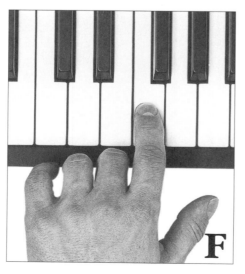

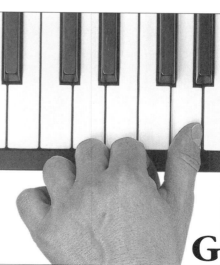

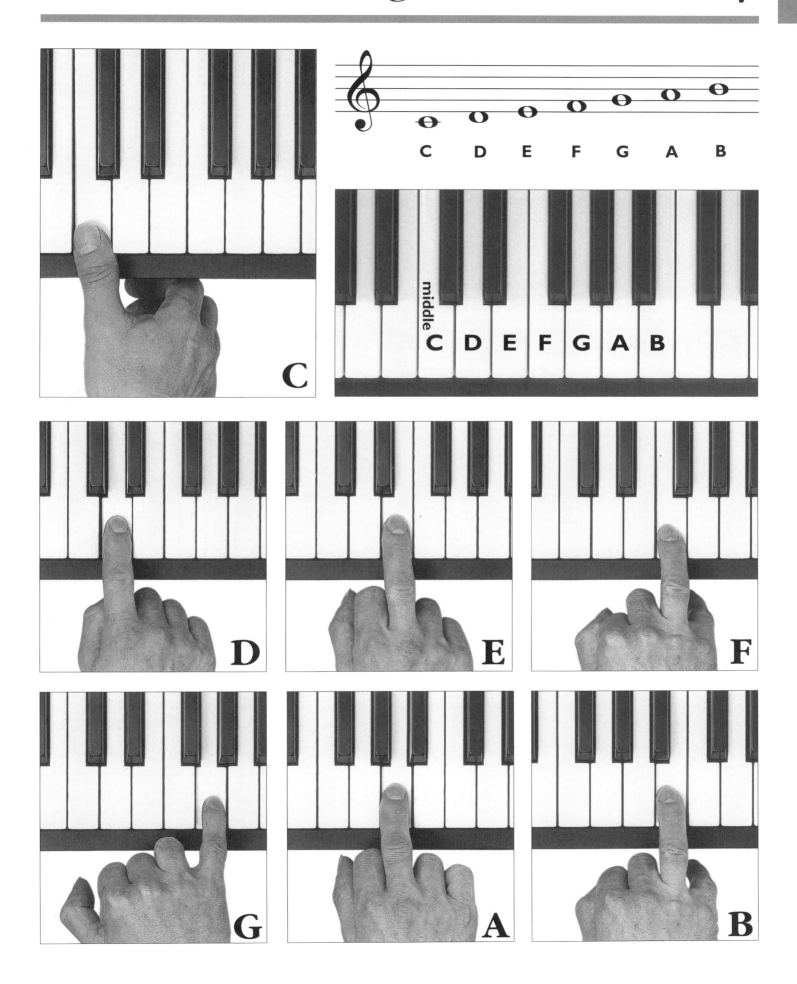

Chords

A chord is created when you play more than one note simultaneously. You can do this with the right or left hand, or with both at once. There are many different types of chord, but here are a few simple shapes you can master in seconds.

Right-Hand Chords

Most notes in a chord are played with the right hand. Later we will add more notes to our chords and introduce the left hand.

C major

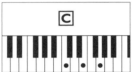

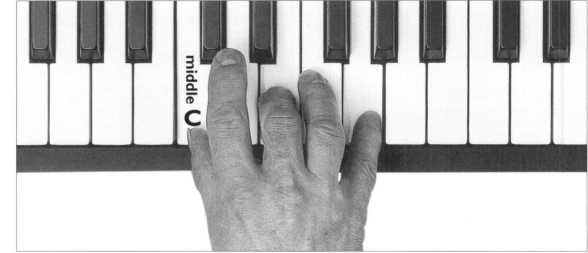

F major

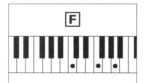

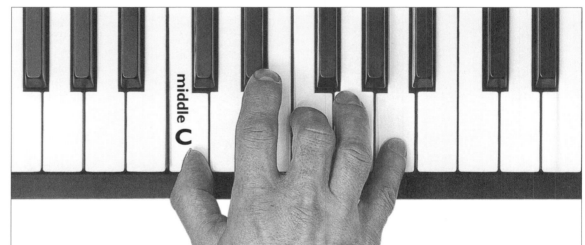

G major

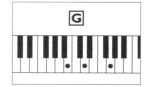

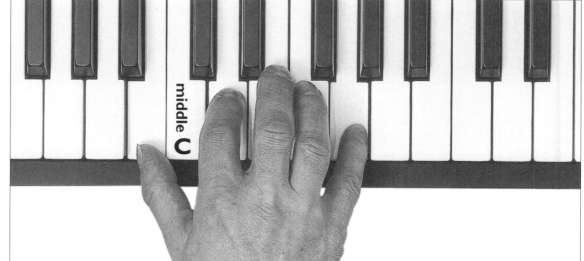

Your fingers won't always lie from 1 – 5 over C – G in the right hand, and this chord sequence is a case in point. To move to the best position in the second bar, it is necessary to prepare in bar 1, so you should use fingers 1, 2, and 4 to play the first chord.

When the same chord comes back in bar 5 you can use the standard 1, 3, 5 fingering, because this helps prepare the downward movement for the chord in bar 6. Try to make the fingers move smoothly and positively from one key to another.

As you play one chord, try to think ahead to the next one, and prepare your fingers for their new positions.

Listen to the demonstration on **Track 13**, and then try playing along with the backing on **Track 14**.

Tip

Try not to let your hands move out of position when you play this piece—as the music gets more complex it's increasingly important that your hands make the minimum movement to play the notes.

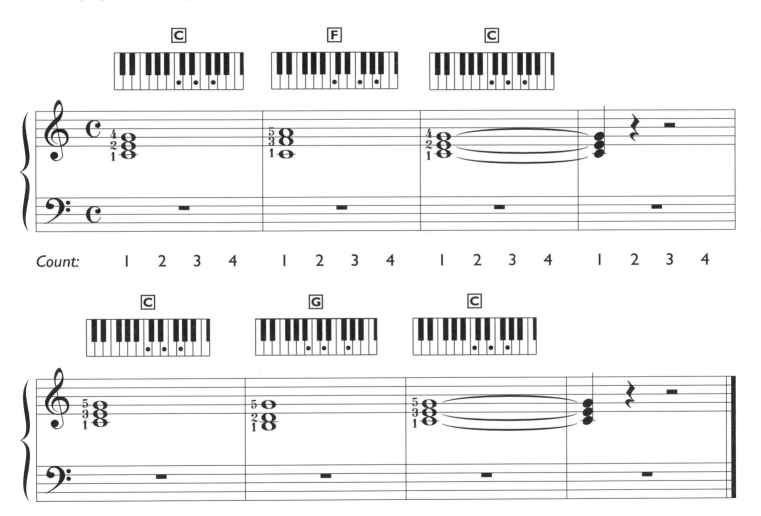

Chords with both hands

Now let's add the left hand. Generally, when playing chords, the left hand plays fewer notes than the right, and they are more widely spaced. The left and right hands don't play separate chords, they simply share the job of playing the notes of one chord.

Tip

If you have a tempo control on your keyboard, use it to learn the pieces at a slower speed; then you can gradually come up to the proper speed.

Practice the following exercise one hand at a time. You already know the right hand part, as it's exactly the same as the previous exercise. Now we are going to add the left hand. Once again, hand and finger positions are crucial—you should be able to play this exercise without dramatically moving your hand up and down the keys. From the one basic hand position you have been using so far you should be able to play all the notes in this piece.

Listen to the demonstration on **Track 15**, and then try playing along with the backing on **Track 16**.

C major

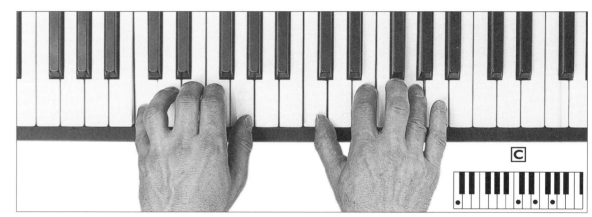

F major

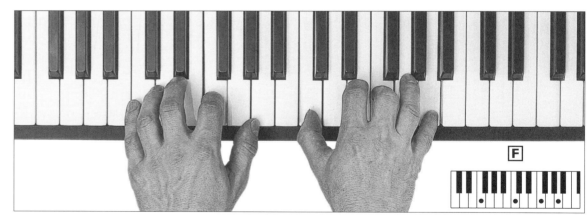

G major

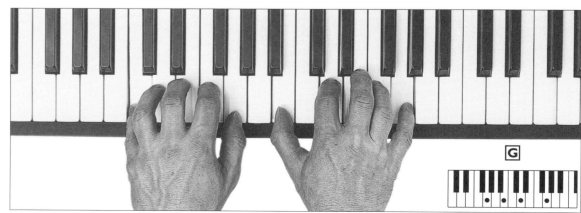

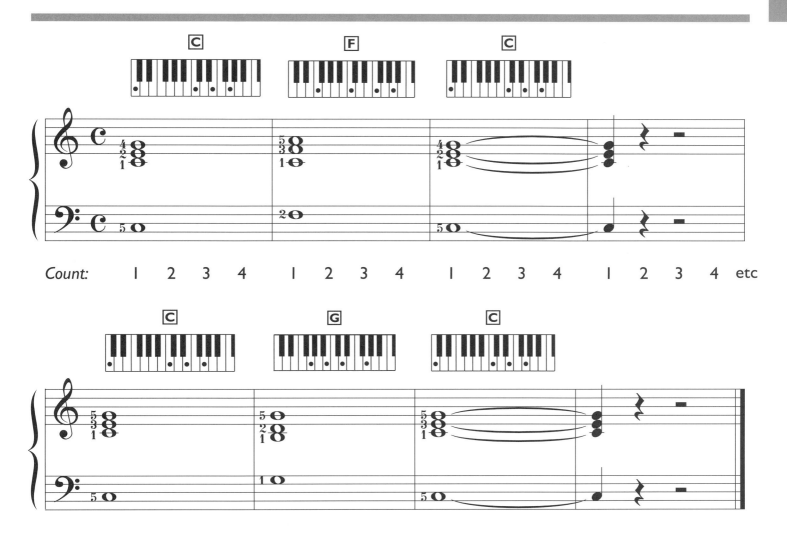

Count: 1   2   3   4   1   2   3   4   1   2   3   4   1   2   3   4   etc

Make sure you are familiar with not only the names of the notes we have learned so far, but also with their position on the keyboard, and what they look like when written on the staff in both bass and treble clefs. If you can do this you are well on your way to being able to read music.

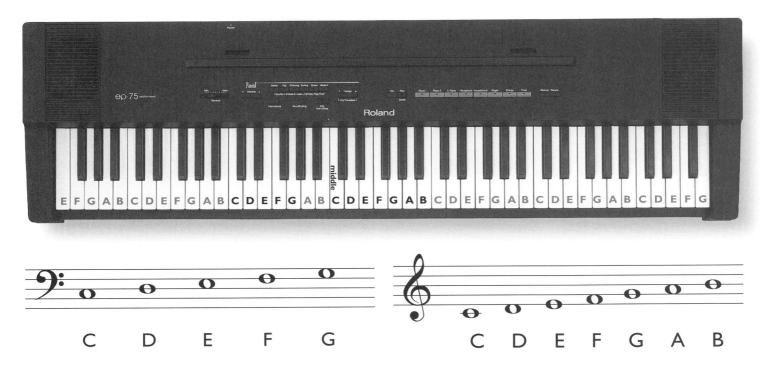

C   D   E   F   G   C   D   E   F   G   A   B

Moving the right hand

Now let's try a little motion in the right hand, while keeping the left hand steady. Remember that the quarter notes in the right hand have a count of one beat each, while the whole notes have a count of four beats each.

Watch out for the sudden stop at the end. You only play on the first beat of the last bar—the rest of the bar is silent, as indicated by the rests.

As the exercises get more complicated, remember that you can isolate the left and right hands, practicing them independently before putting them together.

Listen to the demonstration on **Track 17**, and then try playing along with the backing on **Track 18**

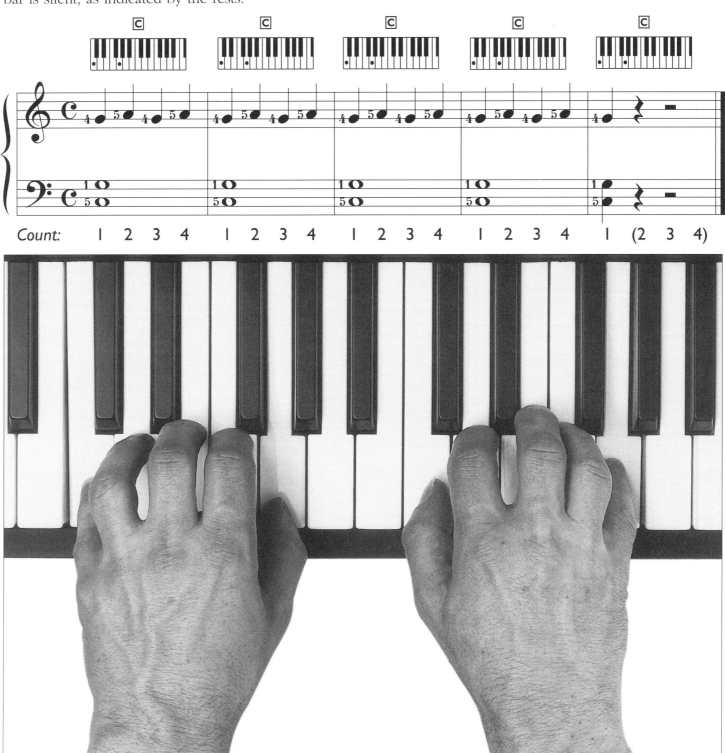

Here's an exercise to get you used to moving your left hand, while keeping your right hand fairly still. The left hand is moving every two beats, so it's quite easy to play, but be careful to keep the note at the bottom of the left hand (C) constant—it's only the upper note that changes.

Listen to the demonstration on **Track 19**, and then try playing along with the backing on **Track 20**.

Tip

Notice that in the last bar you play two beats on and two beats off. Good musicians always try to have tidy endings.

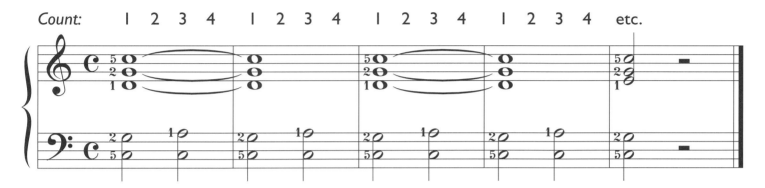

▼ Here's the starting position for the first chord.

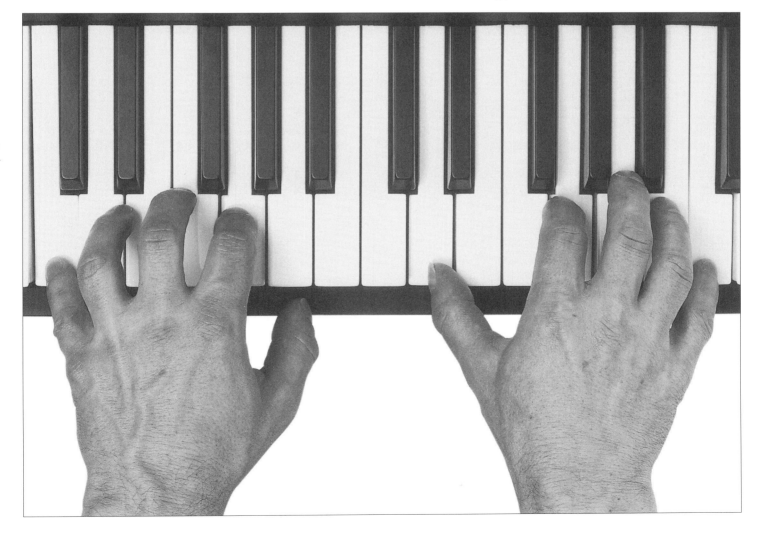

A new note

Now it's time to look at one more note-value, the eighth-note.

Eighth notes are the shortest notes that you're going to play in this book. They last for half a beat and require accurate counting.

How To Count Eighth Notes

Eighth notes split the quarter note beat in half; in a 4/4 bar they are counted like this:

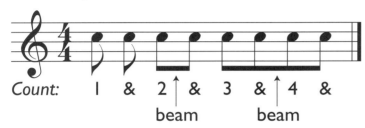

An easy way of remembering the duration of combined eighth notes and quarter notes is (without playing) to call a quarter note 'tea' and two eighth notes "coffee."

Look at the example below and say the words under the staff rhythmically.

Tip

On their own eighth notes are written with a curved flag attached to the stem, but are bracketed together with a beam when groups occur, to make them easier to read.

Next, clap the line as you say the words. Then play the two bars, keeping a steady beat pulse.

Here's a tune full of quarter notes and eighth notes— to practice the rhythm, speak the words (rhythmically); then choose a slow speed and count with a steady beat so you can focus on your fingering. Practice the tune a few times slowly until you can speed up and still be accurate. Look out for the *repeat sign* at the end of the piece.

Repeats

If you see the sign :‖ at the end of a piece, it means that you are to repeat the entire piece. Sometimes only a section of a piece is to be repeated and you will see the sign ‖: at the beginning, and :‖ at the end of that section.

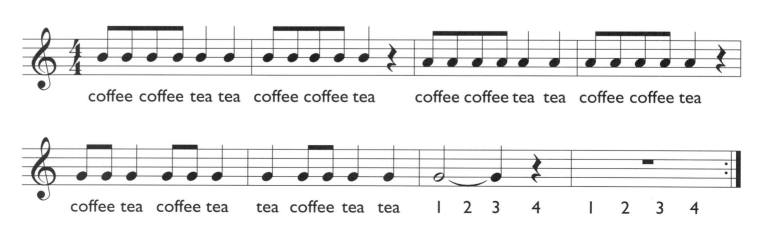

Another common grouping of beats is 3 in a bar. This is sometimes referred to as 'waltz' time.

Count steadily to 3 and keep repeating. Try to feel the emphasis on the first beat of the bar and the rhythm of the tempo.

1 – 2 – 3 / **1** – 2 – 3 / **1** – 2 – 3 / etc

This symbol  is called a dotted half note and lasts for 3 beats. The dot after the half note has the effect of adding half the half note's length to it: you hold the note for 3 beats.

You now have a chance to play four well-known pieces, specially arranged for keyboard. "On Top Of Old Smokey" will be in 3/4 time. Remember to count to yourself before starting, until you feel confident with the rhythm of 3 beats in a bar.

This piece also starts on the last beat of the bar—known as the *upbeat*. This is quite common and you simply need to count 1-2 and then start playing on 3, continuing 1-2-3 from there.

For all pieces, listen to the examples on the CD first, and remember to keep counting all the way through!

Written   Played

| 1 | 2 | 3 | 1 | 2 | 3 | etc. |

Jools Holland has introduced boogie-woogie and R&B piano to a new audience.

CHECKPOINT

WHAT YOU'VE ACHIEVED SO FAR...

You can now:
- Sit comfortably at the keyboard
- Find left and right hand notes on the keyboard
- Read basic note values and pitches
- Read from both the treble and bass clefs
- Play right and left hand chords
- Play left and right hands together

34 Jingle Bells

You're now ready to try playing a complete song!
Remember to follow the music carefully,
and you won't have any problems with this
simple melody.

Keep the left hand steady throughout and concentrate
on getting the melody right.

First listen to **Track 21**, and then try playing along
with **Track 22**.

Traditional

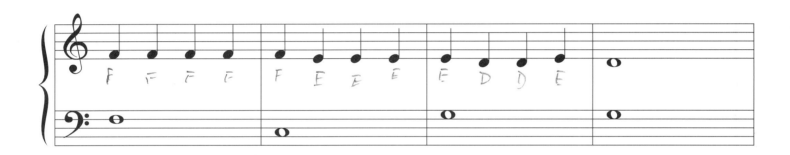

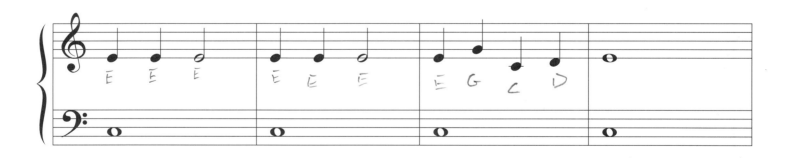

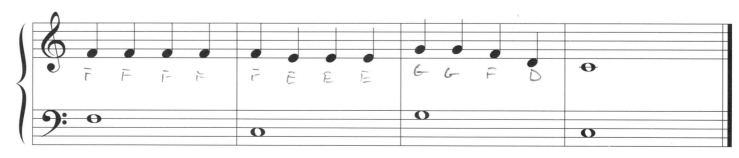

First listen to **Track 23**, and then try playing along with **Track 24**.

We've added chord symbols above the music to help you with the left hand.

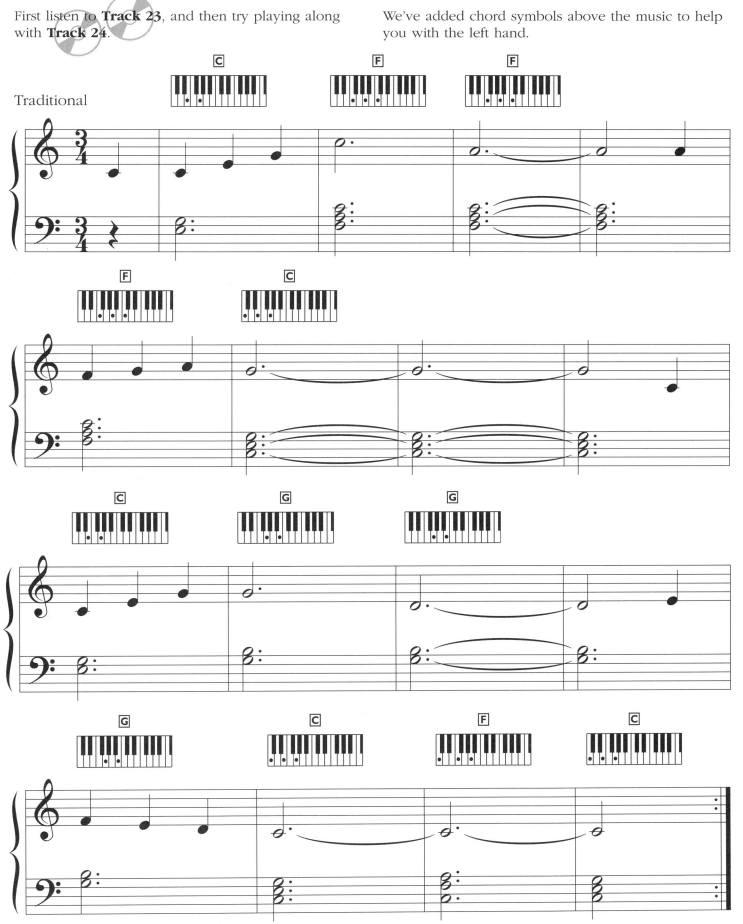

Traditional

Oh When The Saints

Here's another well-known song, to build on your repertoire. Keep the left hand steady, and don't forget to count!

First listen to **Track 25**, and then try playing along with **Track 26**.

Traditional

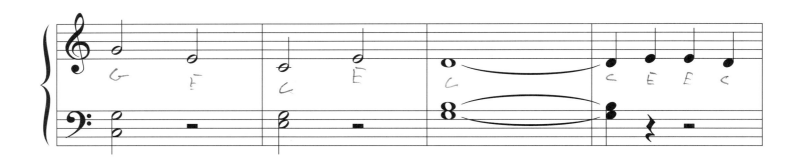

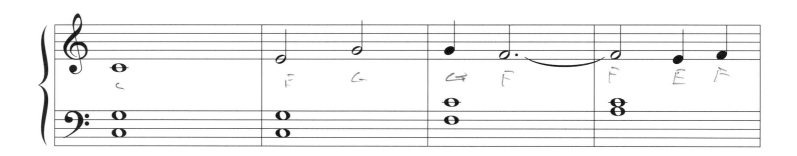

This piece combines everything you've learned so far. You'll need to follow the music quite carefully so your fingers don't end up in knots! Work out fingerings that you are comfortable with, and stick with it - you shouldn't have too many problems.

Listen carefully to **Track 27** and try to follow the music at the same time.

Then play along with the backing track, **Track 28.**

Traditional

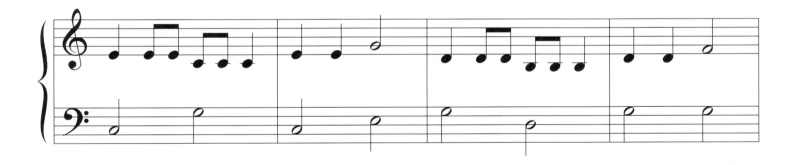

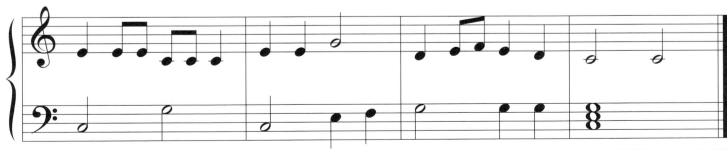

Congratulations!

In a very short span of time you've covered a lot of ground and you're already well on your way to being able to learn and play many more great songs for keyboard.

You've learned correct posture at the keyboard, where to place your fingers on the keys, and how to play with both hands together. You've also learned a lot about music—jhow to read music notation and how to count note lengths and play in time.

We've suggested some songs you might like to try to learn, and also some books to buy to further your knowledge and skills.

Keep up the good work!

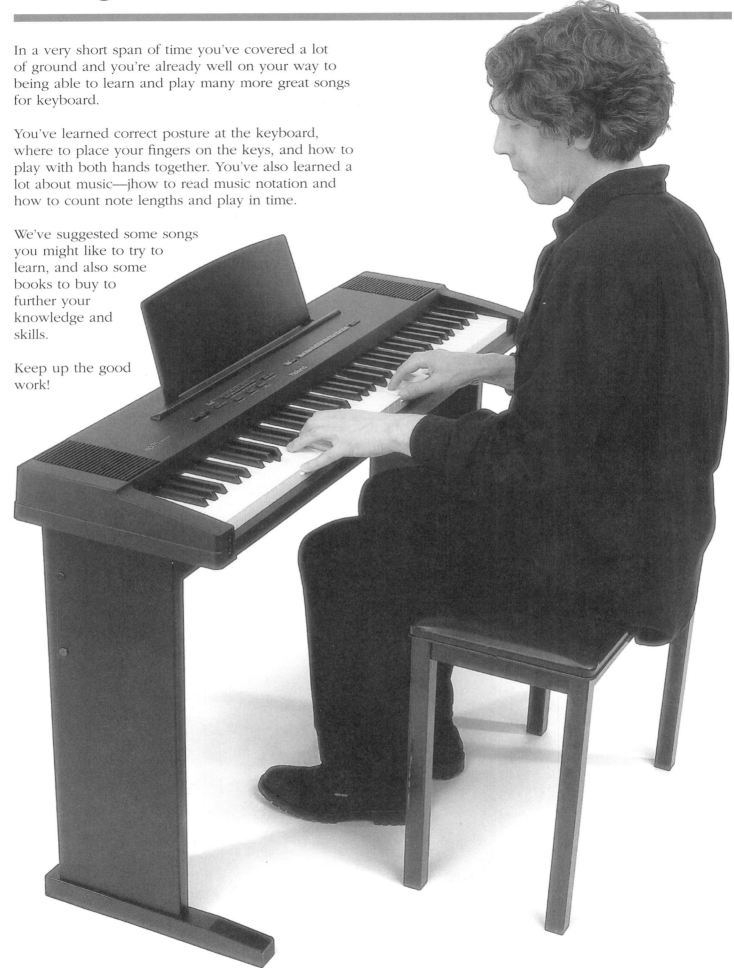

Let it Be The Beatles
Candle In The Wind Elton John
What'd I Say Ray Charles
Bohemian Rhapsody Queen
Imagine John Lennon
Chariots of Fire Vangelis

Light My Fire The Doors
Oxygene Part IV Jean-Michel Jarre
Piano Man Billy Joel
Superstition Stevie Wonder
Theme from 'The Piano' Michael Nyman

Ray Charles

Stevie Wonder

Elton John